YONDE KAITE

よんでかいて

JAPANESE WORKBOOK

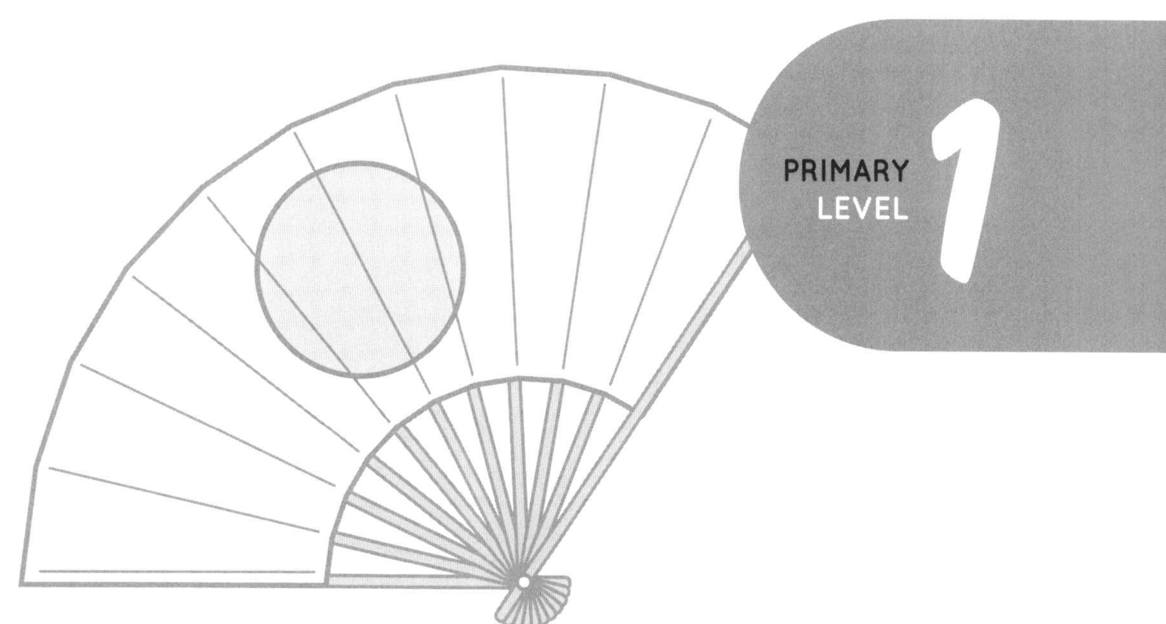

WRITTEN BY

ANNE RAJAKUMAR

WITH ORIGINAL ILLUSTRATIONS BY

JENNIFER CHENG

First published in 1998, reprinted in 2000, 2003, 2004, 2007, 2008, 2010, 2011, 2012, 2016, 2017
This redesigned edition first published in 2017, reprinted in 2019, 2020, 2022, 2023, 2025.

Insight Publications Pty Ltd
3/350 Charman Road
Cheltenham Victoria 3192
Australia

Tel: +61 3 8571 4950
Email: books@insightpublications.com.au

www.insightpublications.com.au

ISBN: 9781875882168

Original illustrations by Jennifer Cheng; other images courtesy of Shutterstock
Cover and internal design by Gisela Beer
Proofing by Sage Napthine-Morrison and Fabrice Wilmann

Printed by Markono Print Media Pte Ltd

Author acknowledgements
Special thanks to my family, Kumar, Timothy and Jessica, for their constant support and assistance and to Barbara and Chris for their untiring advice and unwavering encouragement and help.

Table of Contents

LANGUAGE AND EXTENSION LESSONS

WRITING LESSONS

REVISION LESSONS

ASSESSMENT LESSONS

LL = Language Lesson WL = Writing Lesson

にほんご

☺☺☺ です。	I am ☺☺☺.
こんにちは	hello
さようなら	goodbye

Trace over the hiragana words, then draw a picture of yourself in the frame.
Your teacher will write your name in Japanese for you.

こんにちは。

です。

さようなら。

☺☺☺です。	I am ☺☺☺.
こんにちは	hello
さようなら	goodbye

Here are NORIKO（のりこ）and KENJI（けんじ）.
Trace over their names, then trace over the greetings in their speech bubbles.

What is のりこ saying in English? ______________________________

What is けんじ saying in English? ______________________________

Trace over the word for Japan, then colour in your map.

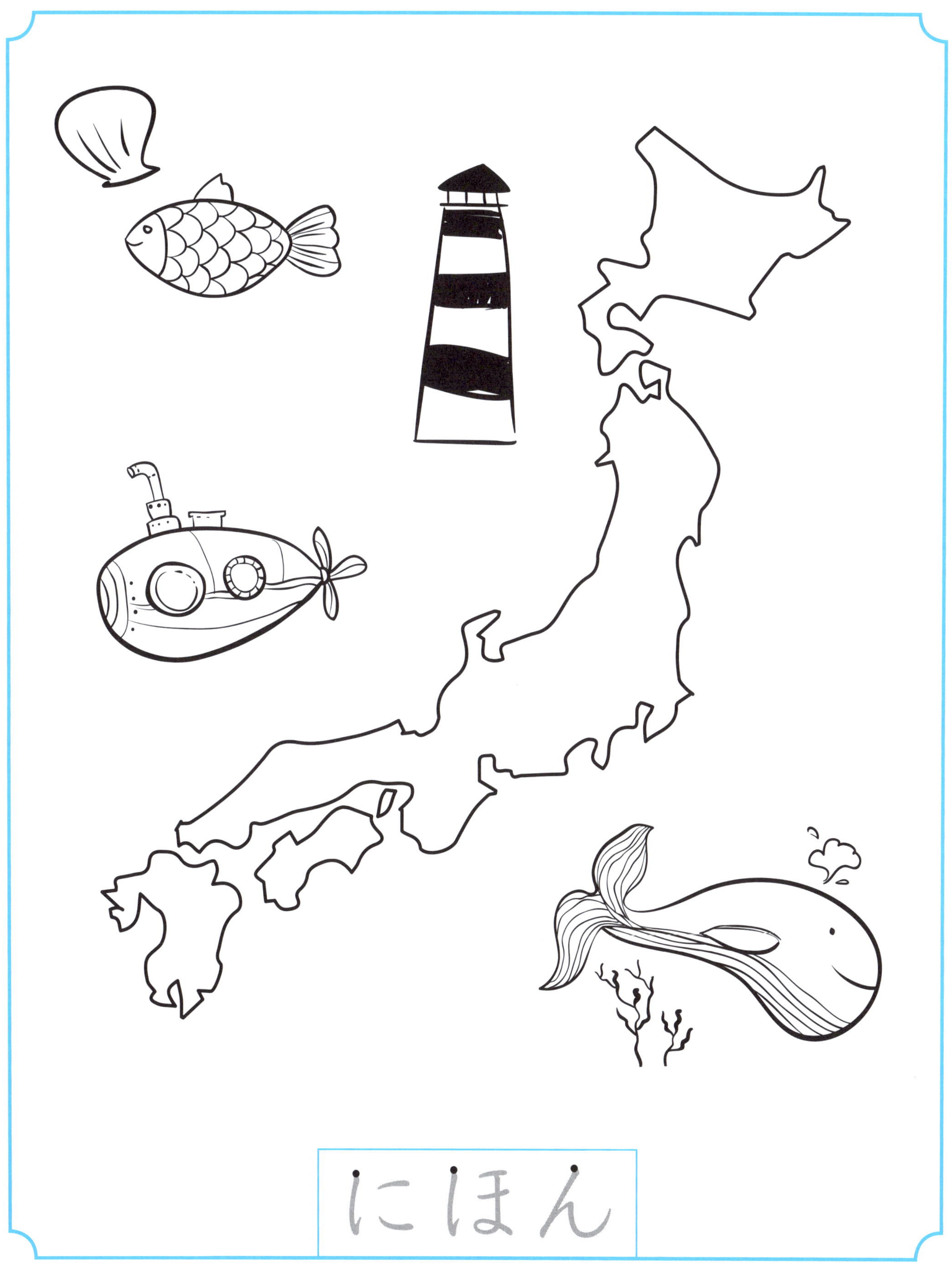

一	1
二	2

三	3
四	4

五	5
六	6

七	7
八	8

九	9
十	10

Write your name in Japanese the correct number of times.

二	
九	
一	
四	
五	
八	
十	
七	
三	
六	

しろ	white
くろ	black

あか	red
あお	blue

きいろ	yellow

Trace over the hiragana words, then shade each oval in its correct colour.

しろ	white
くろ	black

あか	red
あお	blue

きいろ	yellow

Colour in the correct colours.

Trace over the words of the body song, then trace over the labels underneath the pictures.

THE BODY SONG

(to the tune of London Bridge)

あたま　かた　ひざ　あし

ひざ　あし

ひざ　あし

あたま　かた　ひざ　あし

め　みみ　くち　はな

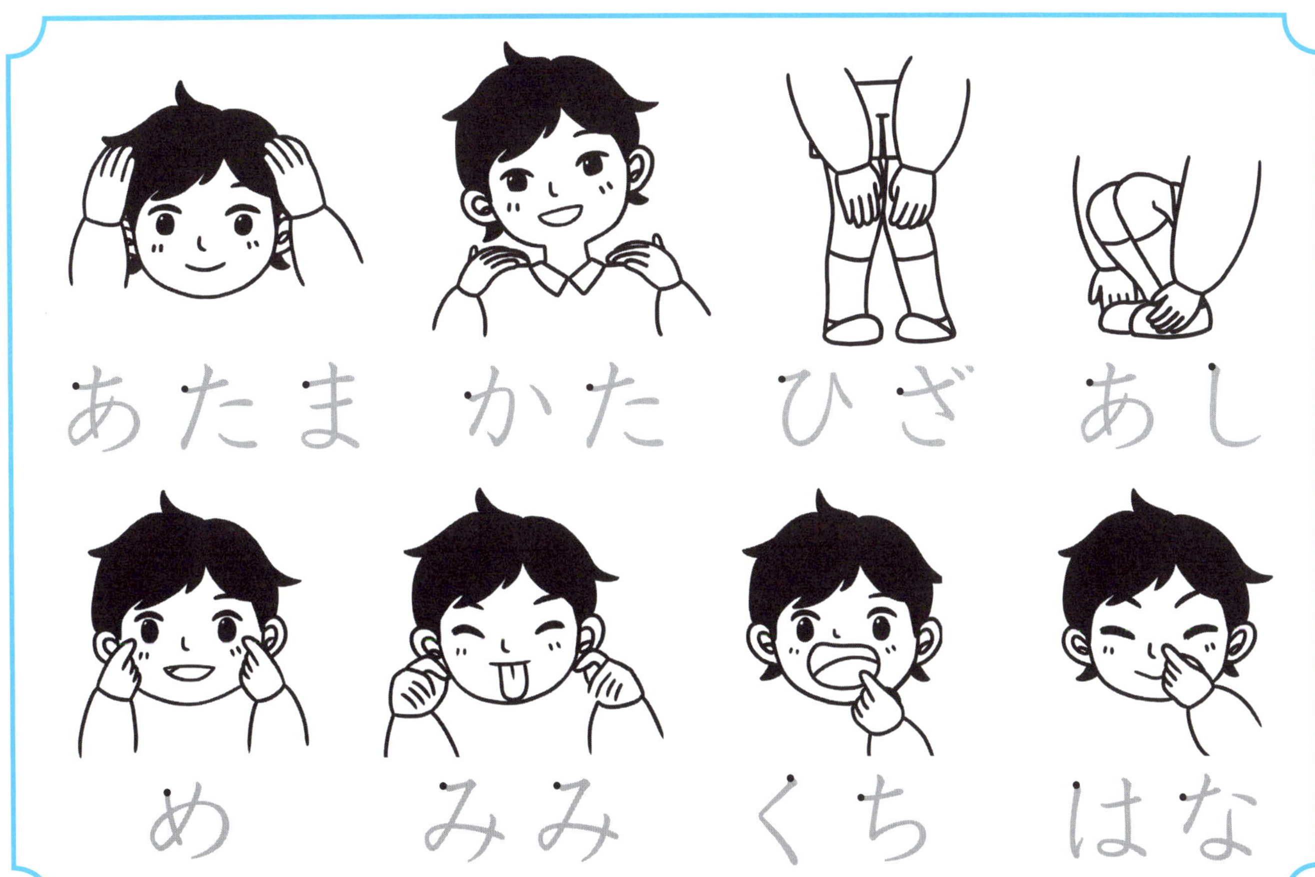

あたま	head
かた	shoulders
ひざ	knees

あし	legs
て	hands
おなか	tummy

Trace over the correct label, then colour in your picture.

め	eyes
みみ	ears
くち	mouth

はな	nose
かみのけ	hair

Draw in the missing face parts, then trace over the Japanese labels. Join your labels to the matching part of your picture with a line.

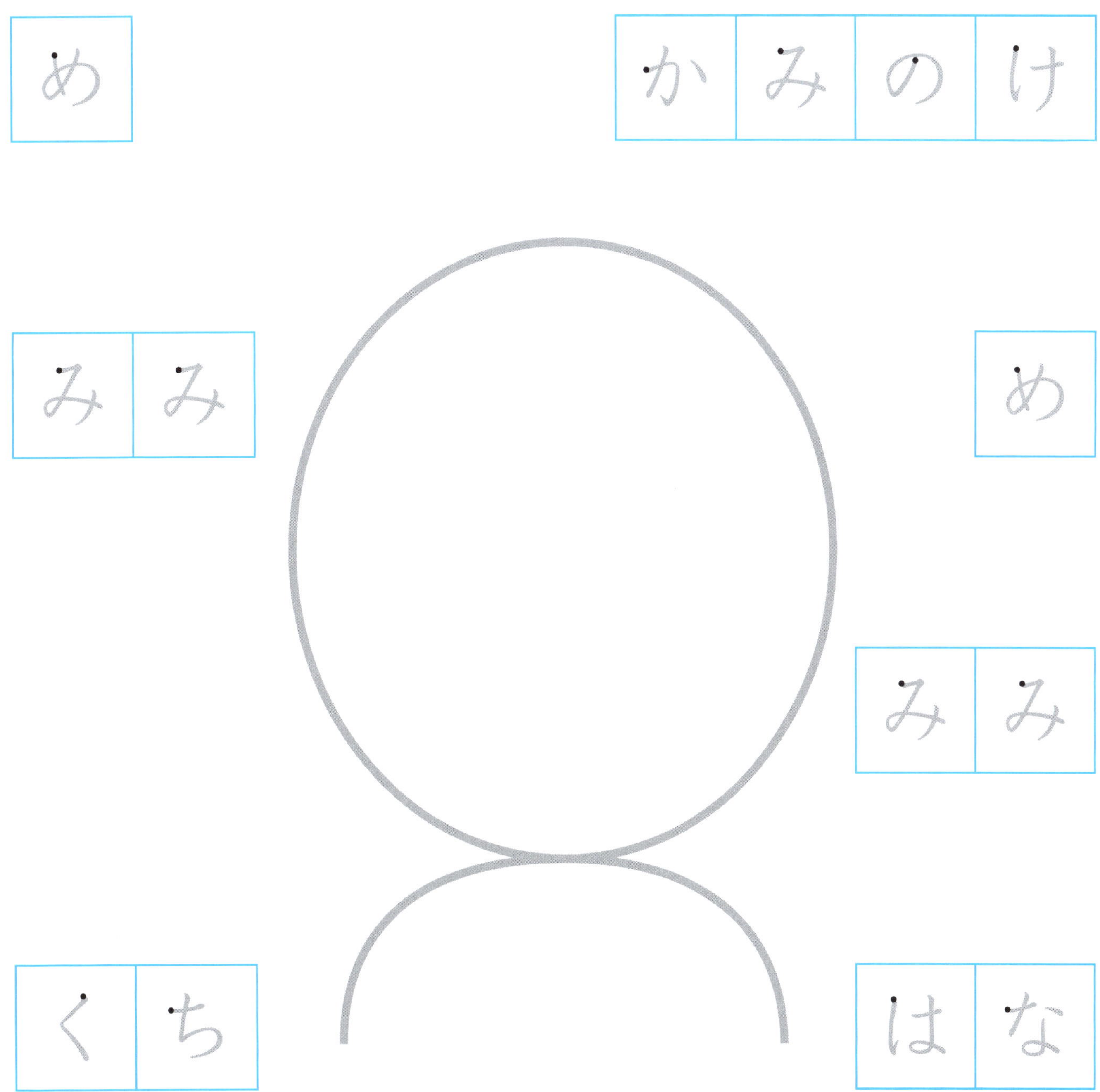

あたま	head
おなか	tummy
あし	legs
て	hands

あか	red
あお	blue
きいろ	yellow
しろ	white
くろ	black

Draw an alien. Use the following colours for each body part.

あたま	あか
おなか	きいろ

あし	あお
て	くろ

スカート	skirt	ズボン	pants
シャツ	shirt	くつした	socks
ワンピース	dress	くつ	shoes

Trace over the Japanese words below, then draw a picture in each box to match the label.

ワンピース	くつ
くつした	シャツ
ズボン	スカート

スカート	skirt	ズボン	pants
シャツ	shirt	くつした	socks
ワンピース	dress	くつ	shoes

Trace over the Japanese words below, then join the clothes to the matching labels.

LANGUAGE LESSON 7 THE CLASSROOM

ほん	book
かみ	paper
えんぴつ	pencil

いす	chair
つくえ	desk
せんせい	teacher

Colour the matching words and pictures the same colour, then join them with a line.

ほん	book	いす	chair
かみ	paper	つくえ	desk
えんぴつ	pencil	せんせい	teacher

Trace over the hiragana letters and words, then fill in the missing boxes to complete the labels.

LANGUAGE LESSON 8 BIG AND SMALL

おおきい	big

ちいさい	small

Which of these things are おおきい and which are ちいさい ?

Trace over the correct Japanese word, then colour in the picture.

おおきい	ちいさい

おおきい	ちいさい

おおきい	ちいさい

おおきい	ちいさい

おおきい	big

ちいさい	small

Collect the hiragana letters along the correct way to the castle. What word do they spell?

Japanese: ☐☐☐☐ English: ☐

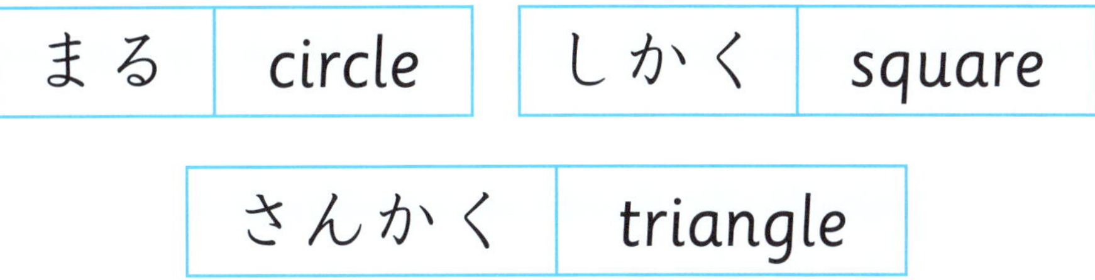

Trace over the shape words in the picture ONLY IF THEY ARE CORRECT.

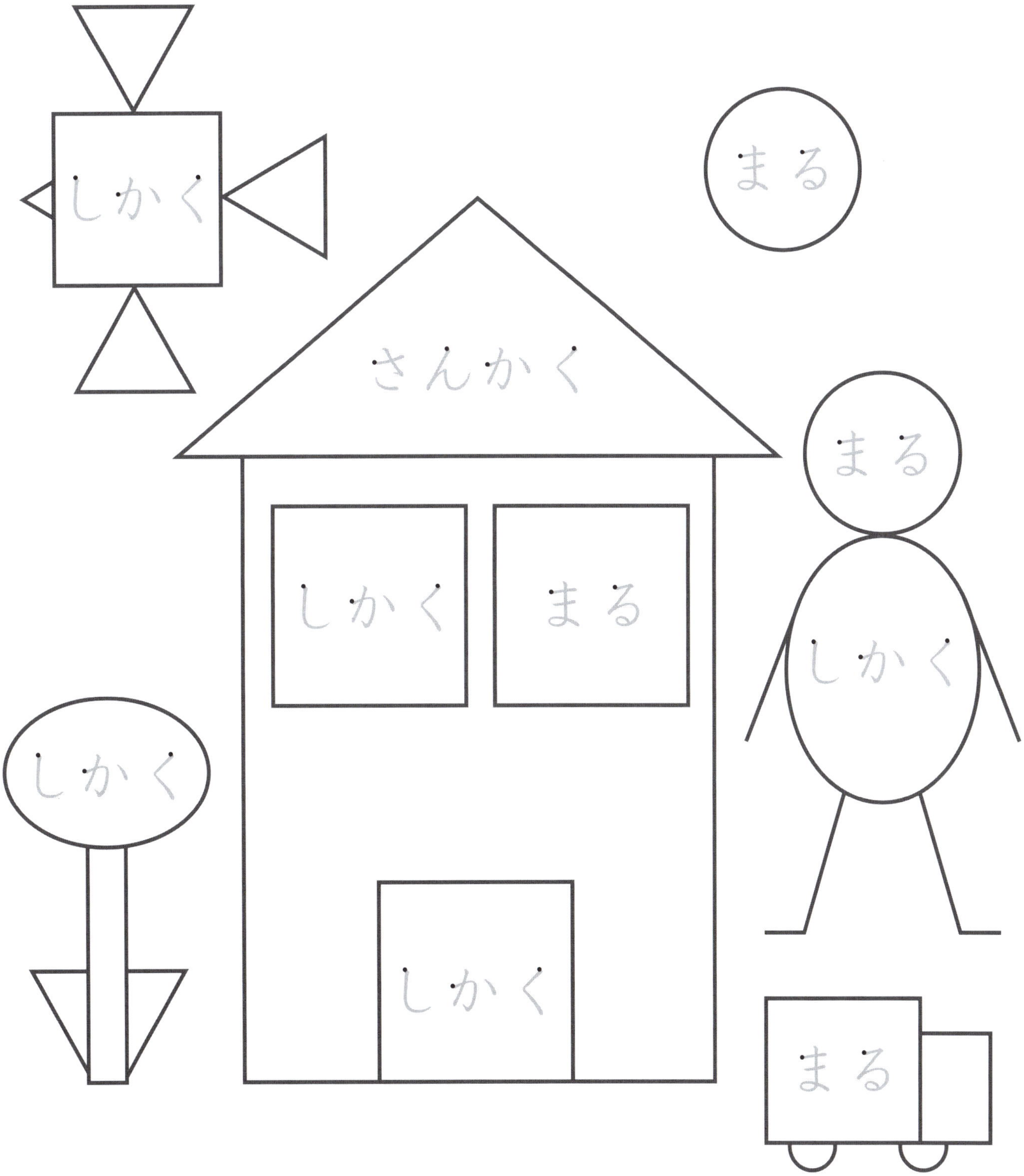

しかく

まる

さんかく

まる

しかく

まる

しかく

しかく

しかく

まる

一	1
二	2
三	3
四	4
五	5

六	6
七	7
八	8
九	9
十	10

さんかく	triangle
しかく	square
まる	circle

Trace over the shape words, then draw the correct number of shapes in each row.

七	まる	
四	さんかく	
五	まる	
一	しかく	
八	さんかく	
二	しかく	
九	さんかく	
三	しかく	
六	まる	
十	さんかく	

おかあさん	mother

おとうさん	father

Draw a picture of an おかあさん and an おとうさん, then trace over the labels.

おかあさん

おとうさん

おとうさん	father
おかあさん	mother

あか	red
きいろ	yellow

Colour the shapes with おとうさん in きいろ

Colour the shapes with おかあさん in あか

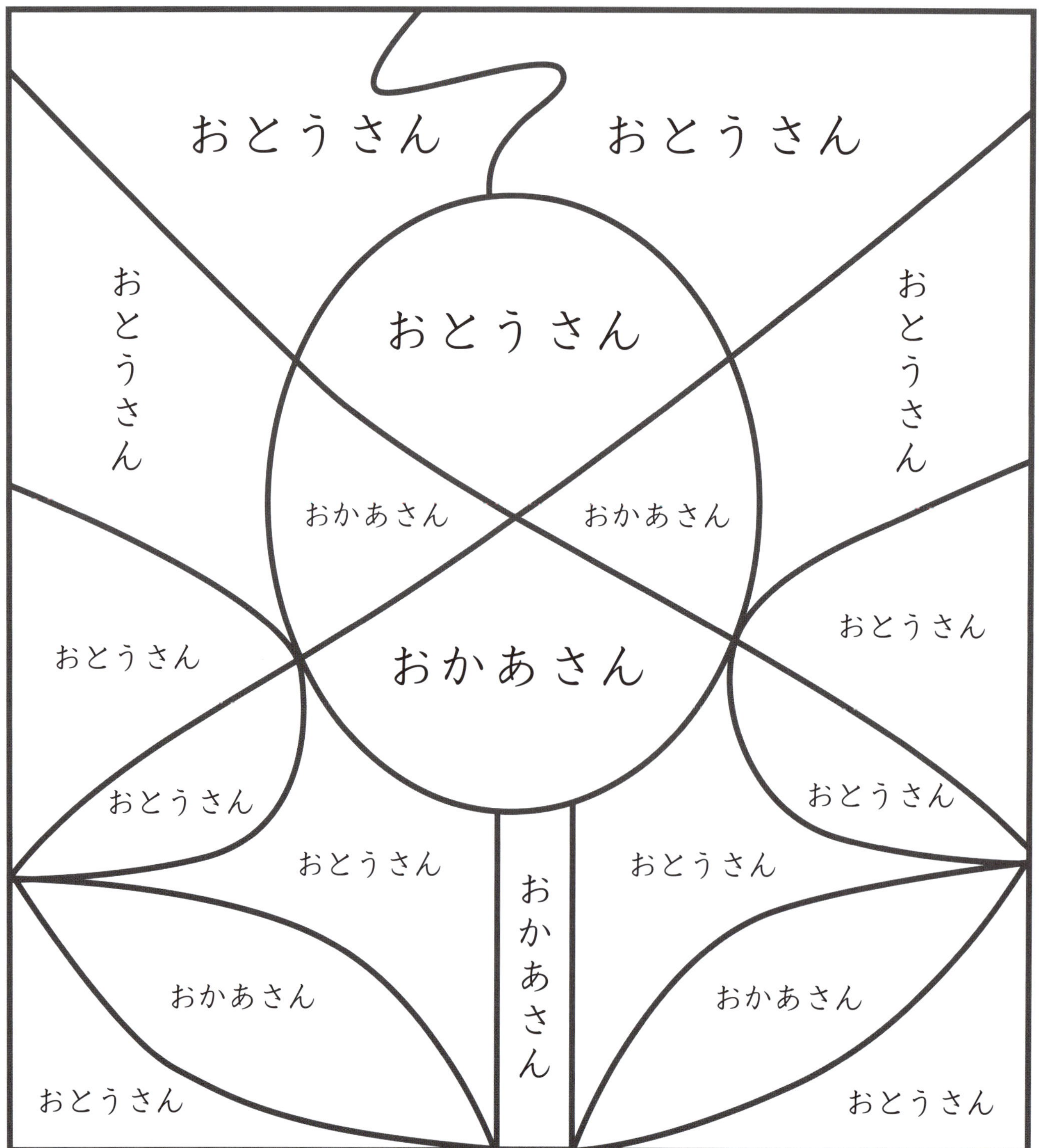

ぼくの	my (used by boys)
わたしの	my (used by girls)
いえ	house

Make an origami house and paste it in the square below. Trace over the label under your picture.

If you are a girl, trace over the girl's word: わたしの

If you are a boy, trace over the boy's word: ぼくの

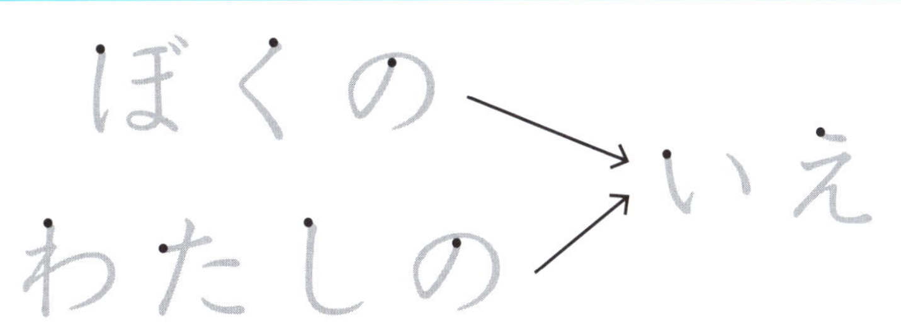

Practise your hiragana letters, then use them to make a picture of anything you like in the box provided.

KU	く	く	く	く	
	く				
SHI	し	し	し	し	
	し				
SO	そ	そ	そ	そ	
	そ				
TSU	つ	つ	つ	つ	
	つ				
TE	て	て	て	て	
	て				

ベッド	bed	まど	window
ソファー	sofa	ドア	door
テレビ	TV	テーブル	table

1. Trace over and circle the things you have in your bedroom.

テレビ　ソファー　まど

ドア　ベッド　テーブル

2. Trace over the labels, then draw in the missing pictures.

ドア　まど

ベッド　テレビ

ベッド	bed
ソファー	sofa
テレビ	TV

まど	window
ドア	door
テーブル	table

Answer the questions.

What is the English word for テーブル ?

What is the English word for まど ?

What is the English word for ドア ?

What is the English word for テレビ ?

What is the English word for ベッド ?

What is the English word for ソファー ?

Can you remember these hiragana letters? Trace over them, then write the matching romaji in the space provided.

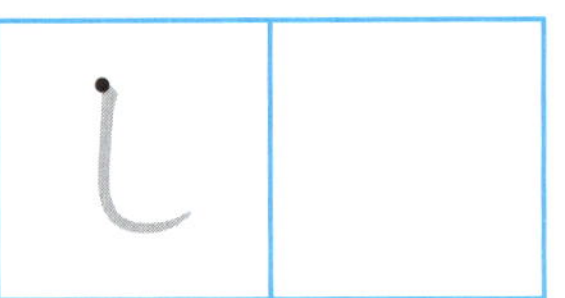
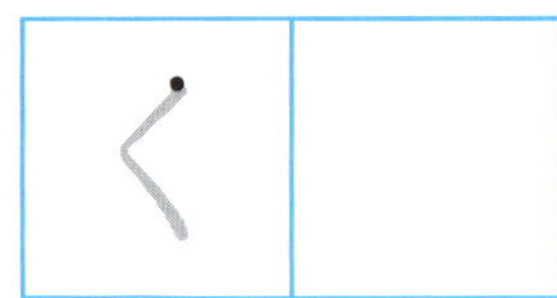
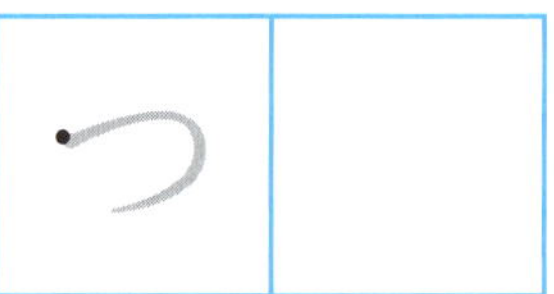
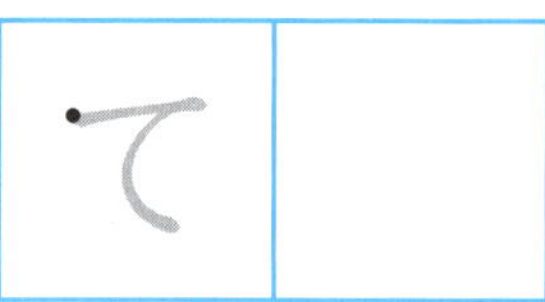
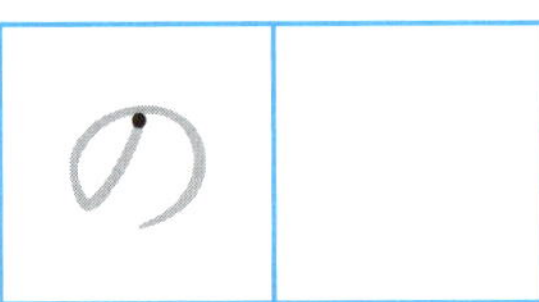

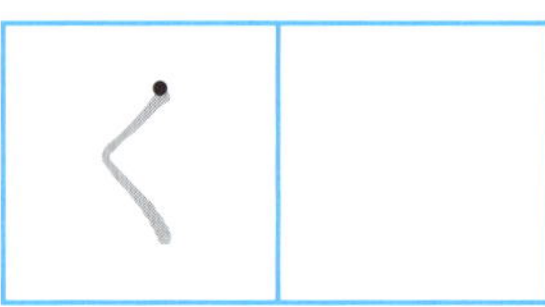
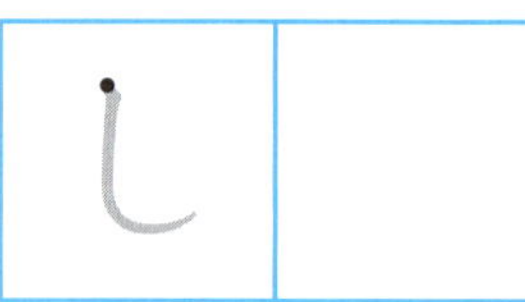

ぶた	pig
うし	cow
いぬ	dog

うま	horse
ねこ	cat
ひつじ	sheep

Trace over the animal words, then join them to the correct pictures with a line.

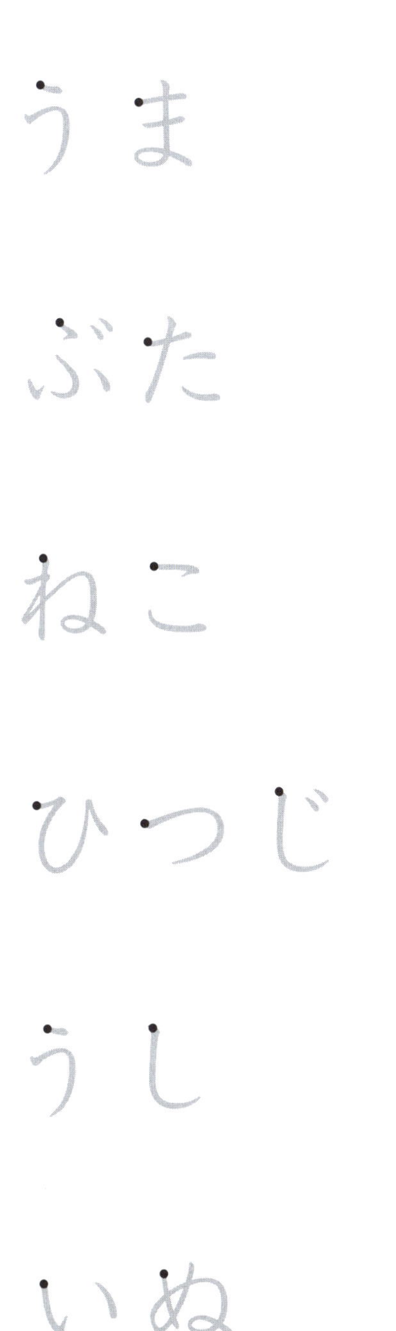

一	1
二	2

三	3
四	4

五	5
六	6

七	7
八	8

九	9
十	10

Join the dots (without using a ruler) to finish the picture, then trace over the label.

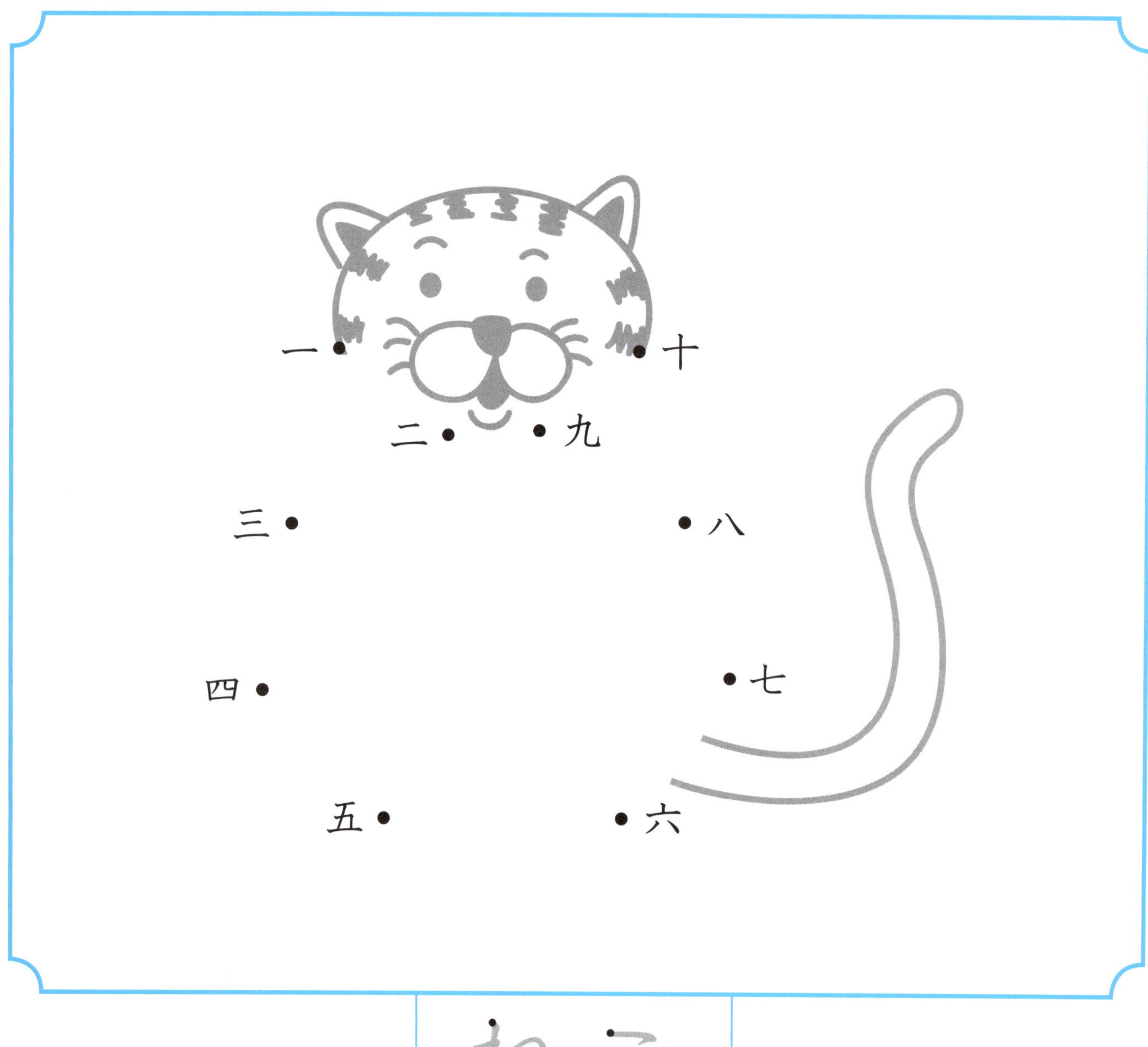

ねこ

ぶた	pig
うし	cow
いぬ	dog

うま	horse
ねこ	cat
ひつじ	sheep

☺☺☺ がすきです。	I like ☺☺☺.

Draw a matching picture in each box. Trace over the grey words in the label to make a sentence for each picture.

ぶた
がすきです。

ひつじ
がすきです。

うし
がすきです。

ねこ
がすきです。

うま
がすきです。

いぬ
がすきです。

ぶた	pig	うま	horse
うし	cow	ねこ	cat
いぬ	dog	ひつじ	sheep

Find and trace over the animal words in the word search. Use your brightest colour for your tracing. Then join each word with its matching picture.

ん	ぶ	た	ひ	う
く	て	の	へ	ま
い	と	か	ね	こ
ぬ	う	そ	ほ	の
ち	し	ひ	つ	じ
む	せ	も	み	は

くるま	car	でんしゃ	train
バス	bus	じてんしゃ	bicycle

Trace over the correct Japanese word, then colour in your picture.

バス	くるま

じてんしゃ	バス

くるま	でんしゃ

バス	くるま

Practise your hiragana letters.

NO	の	の	の	の			
HI	ひ	ひ	ひ	ひ			
HE	へ	へ	へ	へ			
RU	る	る	る	る			
RO	ろ	ろ	ろ	ろ			
N	ん	ん	ん	ん			

Look at the pictures, then draw your own using these hiragana letters.

1	一	一	一	一	一	一
2	一	二	二	二	二	二
3	一	二	三	三	三	三
4	丨	冂	冂	四	四	四
5	一	丆	五	五	五	五

Trace over the kanji numbers, then shade the matching English and Japanese numbers in the same colour and join them with a line.

6	丶	亠	六	六	六	六
7	一	七	七	七	七	七
8	ノ	八	八	八	八	八
9	ノ	九	九	九	九	九
10	一	十	十	十	十	十

Trace over the number kanji.

THE COUNTING SONG
(TO THE TUNE OF JINGLE BELLS)

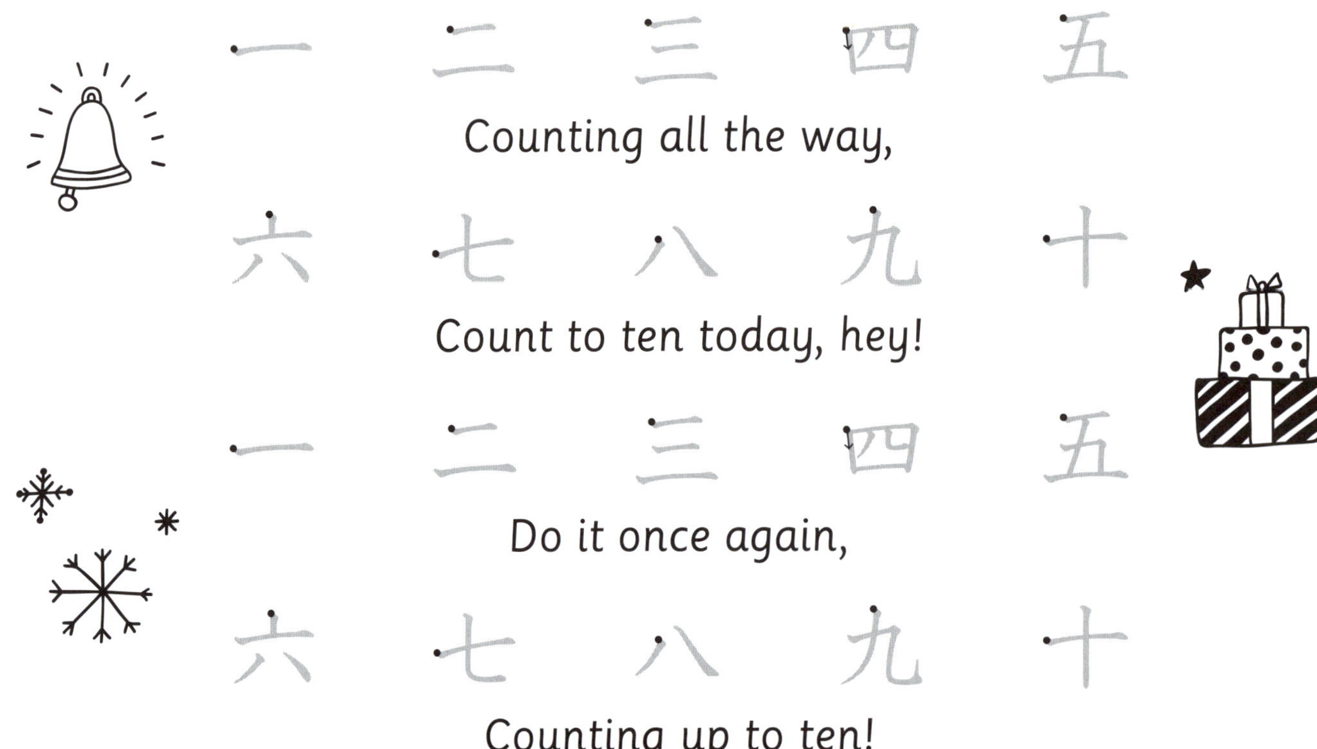

一 二 三 四 五

Counting all the way,

六 七 八 九 十

Count to ten today, hey!

一 二 三 四 五

Do it once again,

六 七 八 九 十

Counting up to ten!

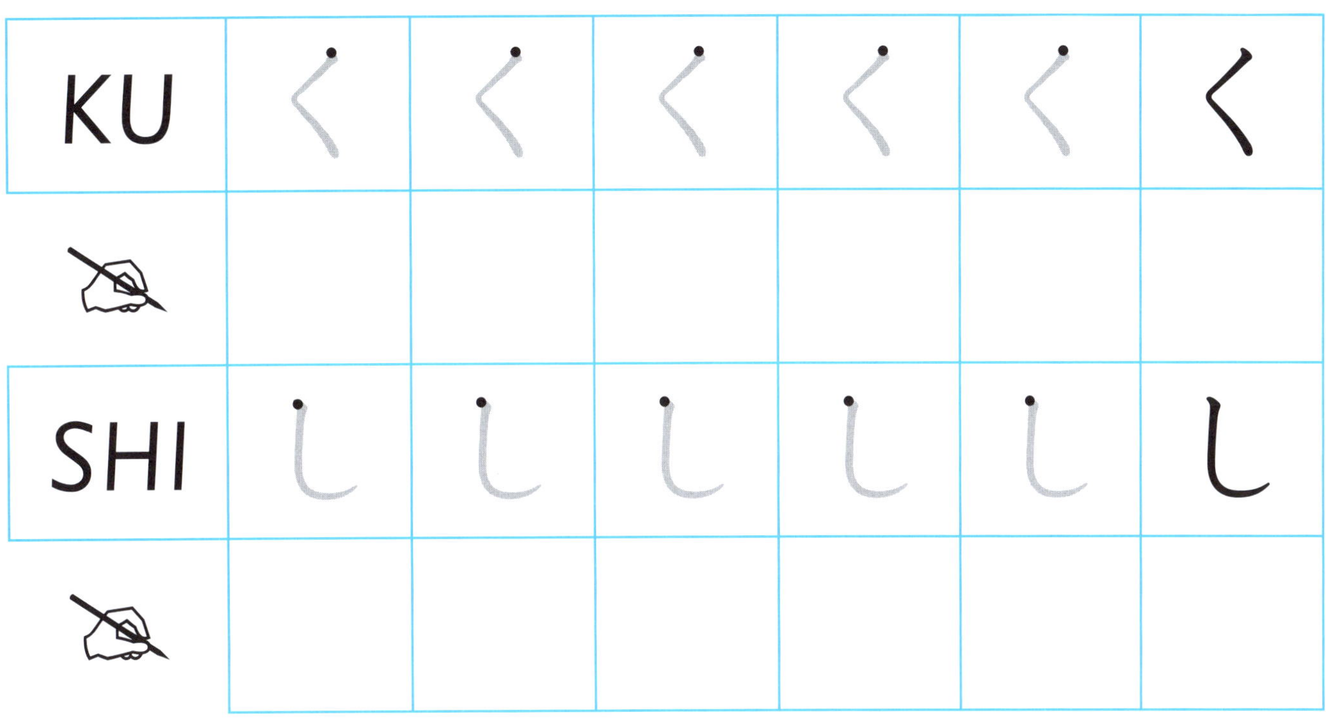

Trace over the hiragana letters, then shade the matching romaji box.

く	KU	SHI
し	KU	SHI
く	KU	SHI
し	KU	SHI
く	KU	SHI
く	KU	SHI
く	KU	SHI
し	KU	SHI

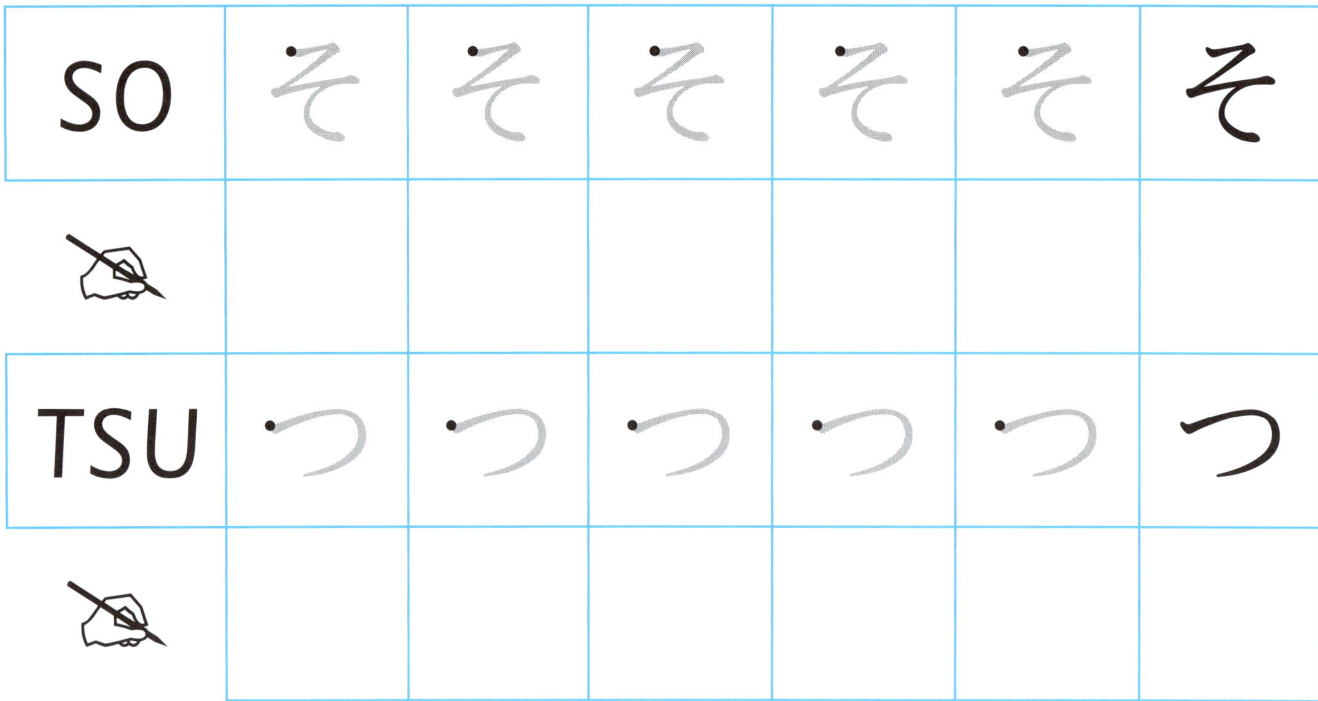

Colour in the shapes which have a そ in your favourite colour.

Colour in the shapes which have a つ in a different colour.

Which hiragana letter have you found?

romaji

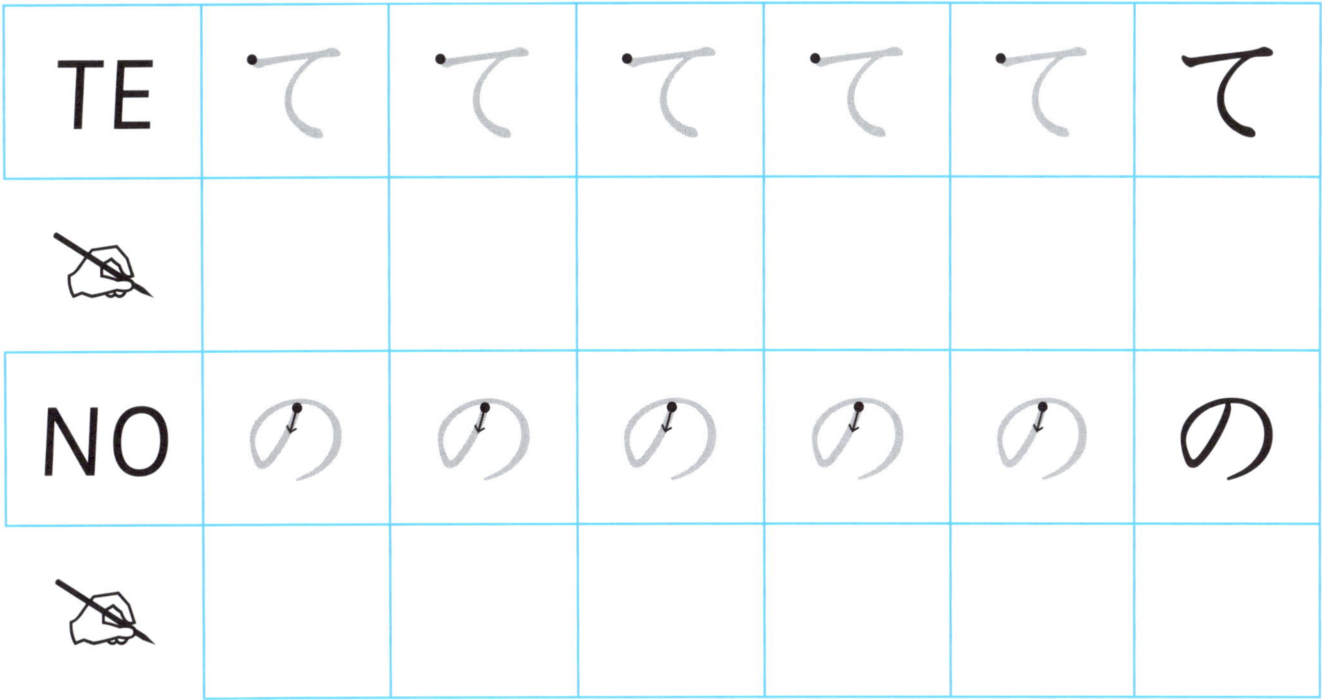

Help the cat catch the mouse by following only the hiragana letter の.

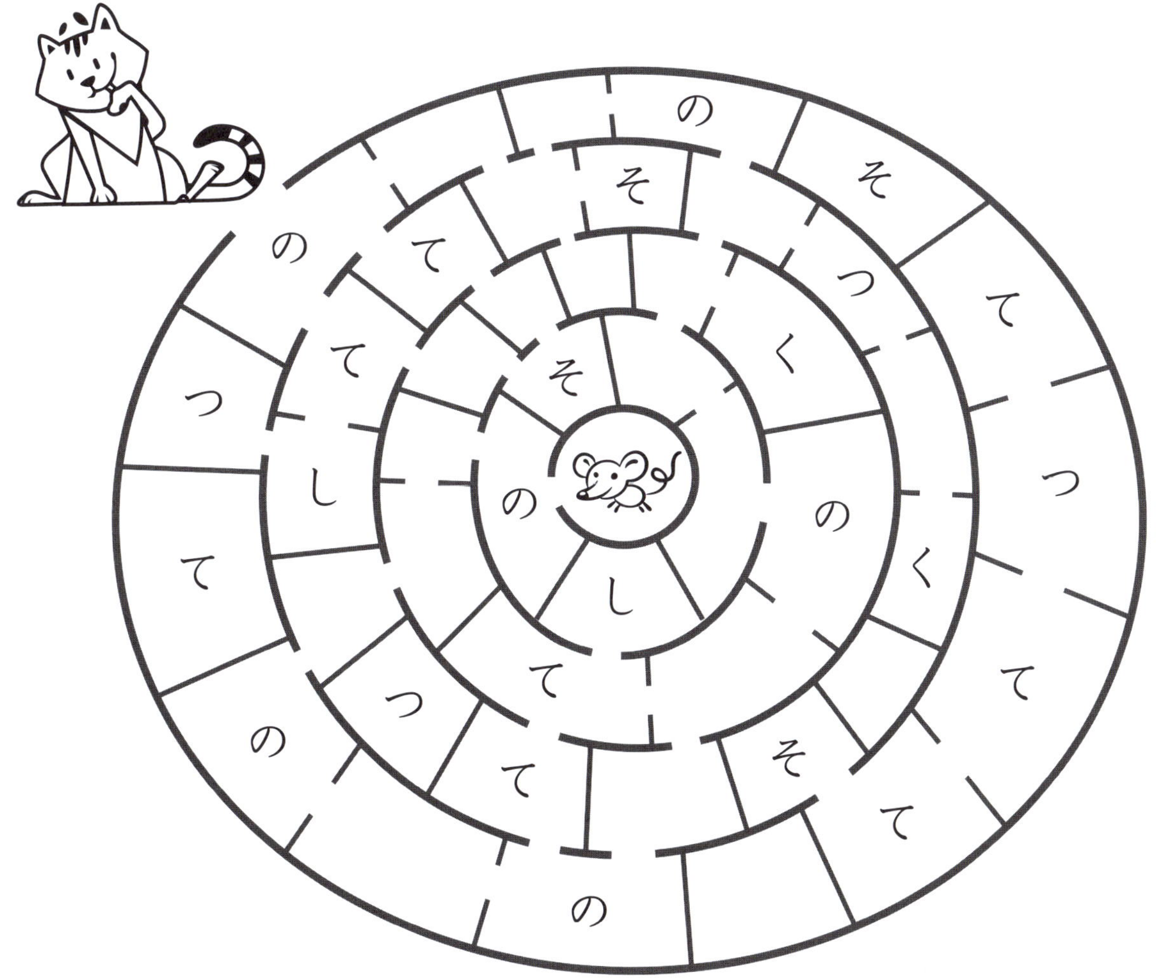

きいろ	yellow
くろ	black

あか	red
あお	blue

Find these hiragana letters in the letter search, then trace over them using the colours given.

そ and つ	きいろ
く and て	くろ

し	あか
の	あお

て	そ	く	と	し	て
こ	た	く	な	そ	の
て	て	さ	し	て	つ
く	の	つ	わ	ぬ	は
そ	て	そ	す	つ	ふ
の	し	く	の	し	に

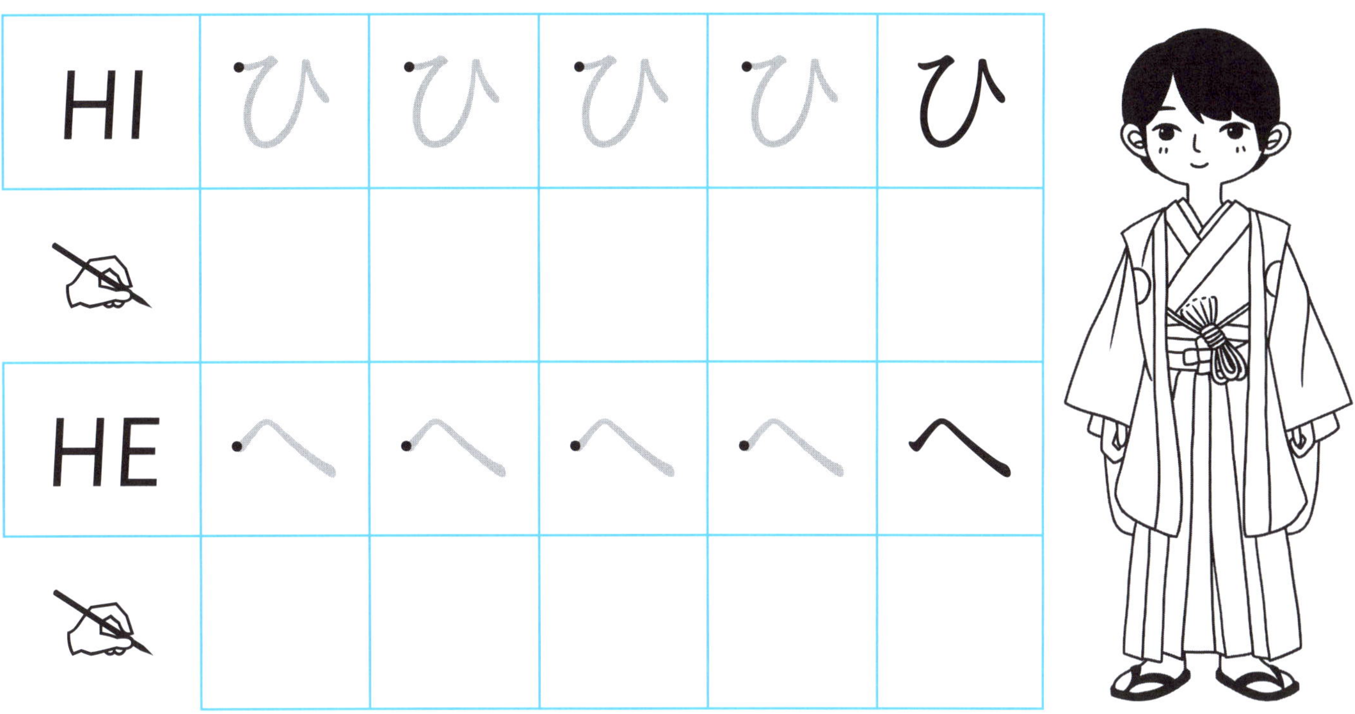

Turn the hiragana letter  into a picture of anything you like.

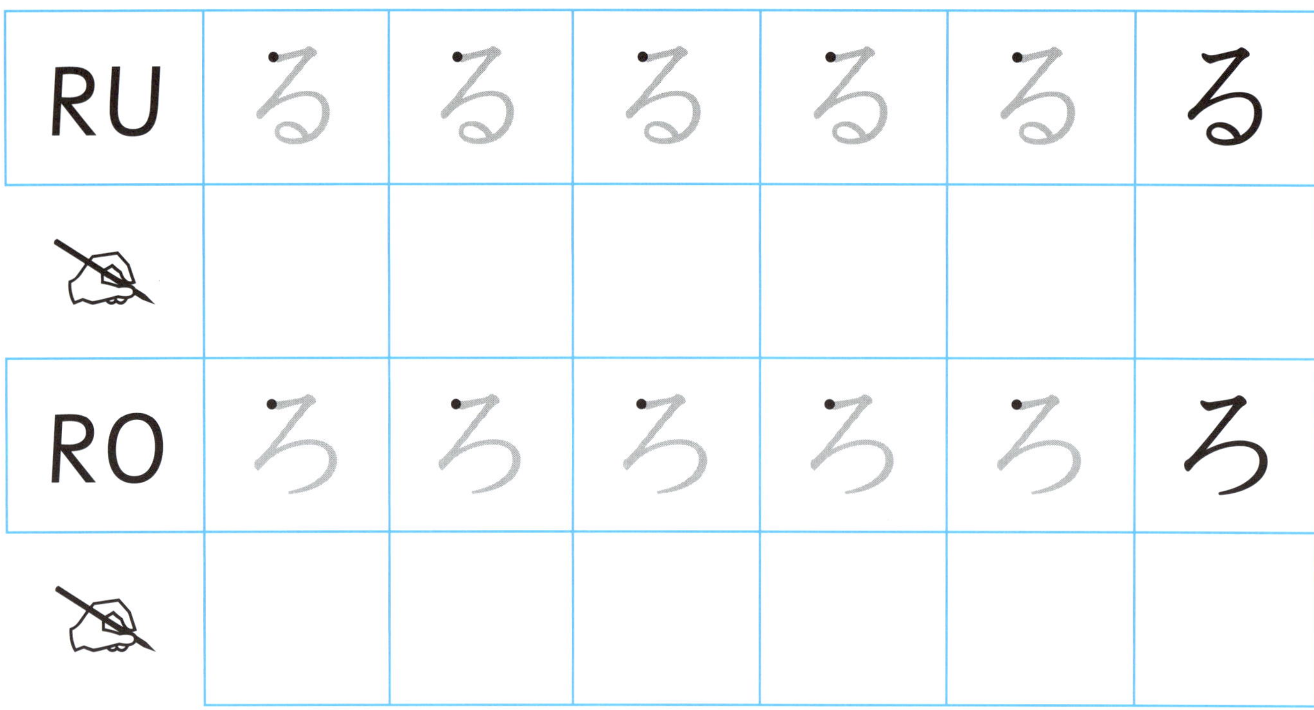

RU	る	る	る	る	る	る
✍						
RO	ろ	ろ	ろ	ろ	ろ	ろ
✍						

Trace over the little hiragana letters to make a big hiragana letter.

ろ ろ ろ ろ ろ
ろ
ろ
ろ ろ ろ
ろ
ろ
ろ ろ ろ ろ

Which hiragana letter have you found?

romaji

N	ん	ん	ん	ん	ん	

How many hiragana letter ん can you find in this picture?

I found ______ hidden ん.

く	KU
し	SHI
そ	SO

つ	TSU
て	TE
の	NO

ひ	HI
へ	HE
る	RU

ろ	RO
ん	N

あか	red
きいろ	yellow

Colour the boxes with matching hiragana and romaji letters in あか

Colour the boxes with different hiragana and romaji letters in きいろ

そ	SO

る	RO

ん	HI

つ	TSU

ひ	HI

の	NO

の	ME

し	KU

し	SHI

ん	N

つ	TE

そ	RO

く	KU

て	TE

る	RU

ん	KU

つ	NO

ん	SO

にほん	Japan
きいろ	yellow
あか	red

あお	blue
しろ	white
くろ	black

Look at the Japanese words we have learned so far. Find them in the word search and trace over them in your favourite colour.

ん	に	ほ	ん	き	て
そ	く	ろ	ま	い	み
あ	お	つ	へ	ろ	あ
そ	の	し	ろ	う	か

Trace over the Japanese words, then use a line to join them with the matching English words.

Japan	きいろ
blue	しろ
white	あか
black	あお
red	にほん
yellow	くろ

一	1
二	2

三	3
四	4

五	5
六	6

七	7
八	8

九	9
十	10

Trace over the kanji numbers, then answer the sums in English or Japanese.

一	+	二	=			五	+	三	=	
三	+	二	=			四	+	四	=	
二	+	四	=			八	+	一	=	
七	+	二	=			六	+	三	=	

Trace over the correct match only.

7	二	六	八	一	九	三	七	十	四	五
9	六	八	一	二	七	四	三	十	四	九
2	五	九	六	四	十	二	一	八	七	三
8	八	一	三	七	六	二	五	四	十	九
3	九	四	六	二	五	三	一	八	七	十
10	三	十	五	七	一	八	七	四	六	二

Circle **one** picture in each box, then follow your teacher's instructions.

REVISION BINGO

あか あお
みどり
くろ

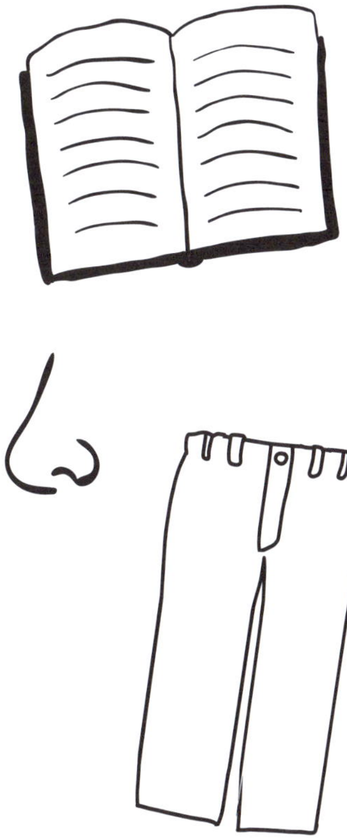

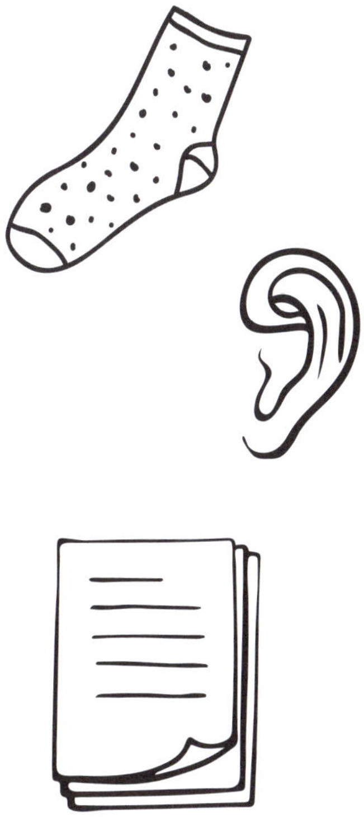

一	1
二	2

三	3
四	4

五	5
六	6

七	7
八	8

九	9
十	10

く	KU	し	SHI	そ	SO	つ	TSU	て	TE	の	NO

Use your brightest colours to trace over the correct letter in each box.

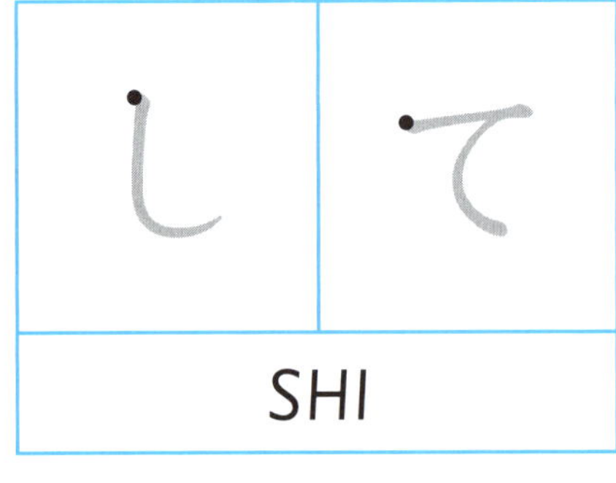
SHI

4

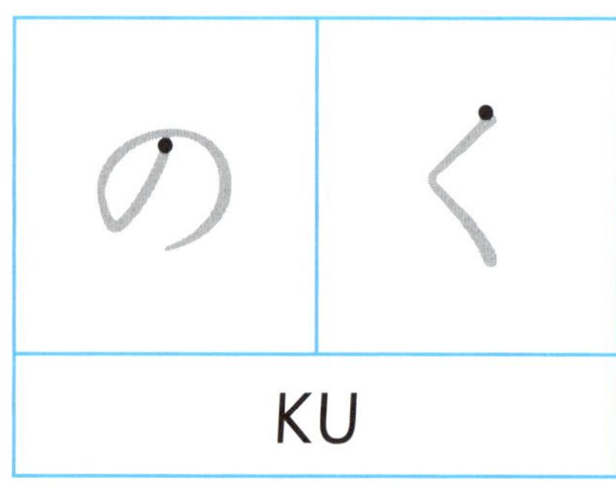
KU

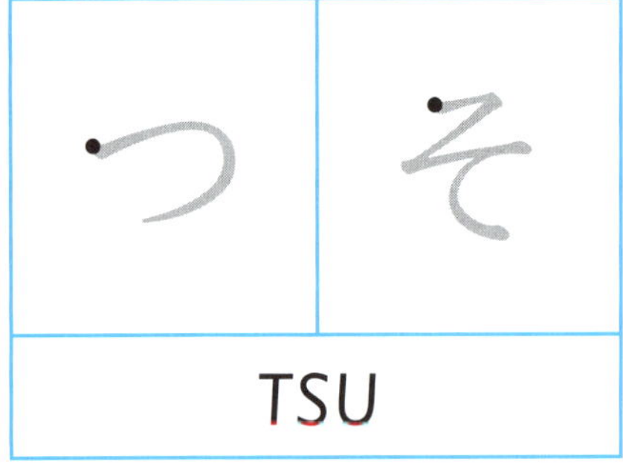
TSU

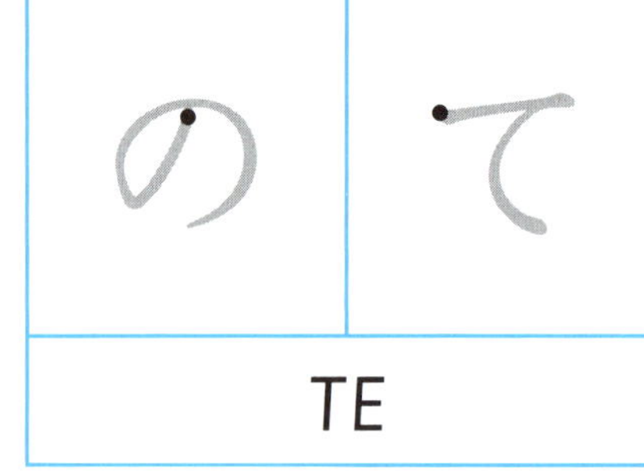
TE

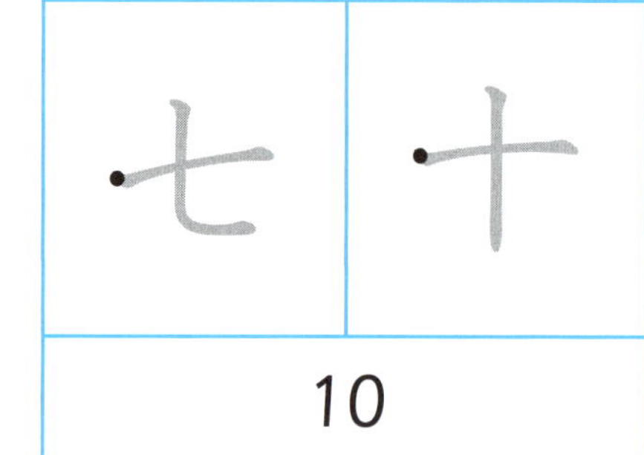
10

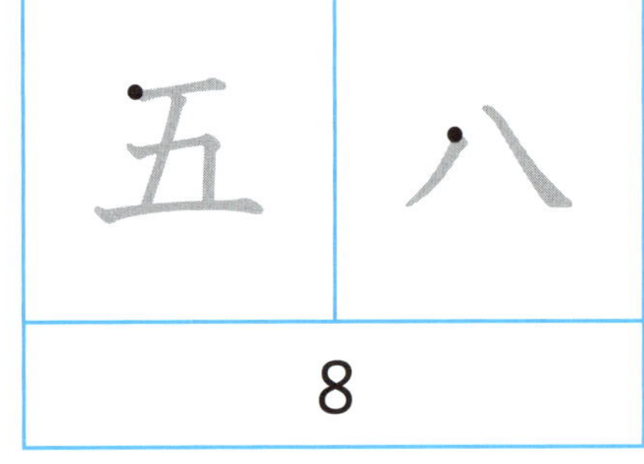
8

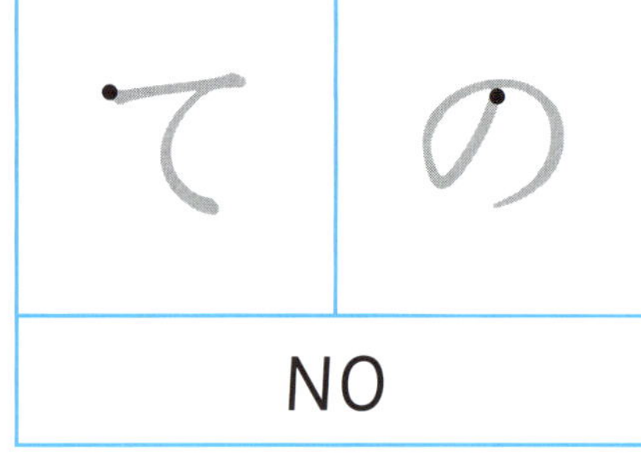
NO

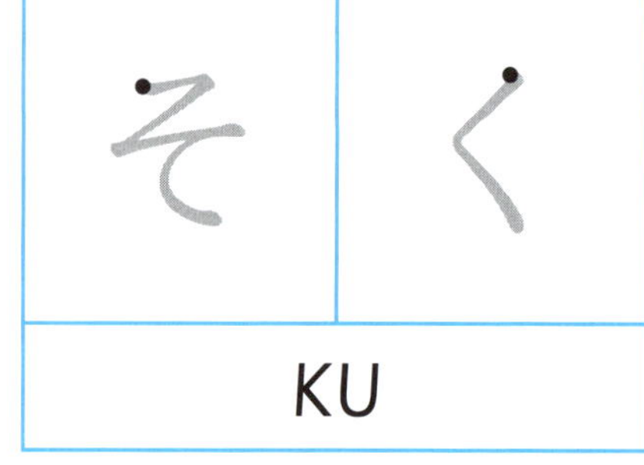
KU

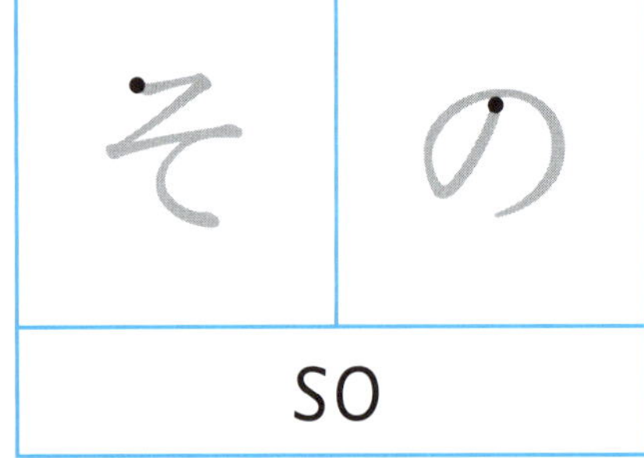
SO

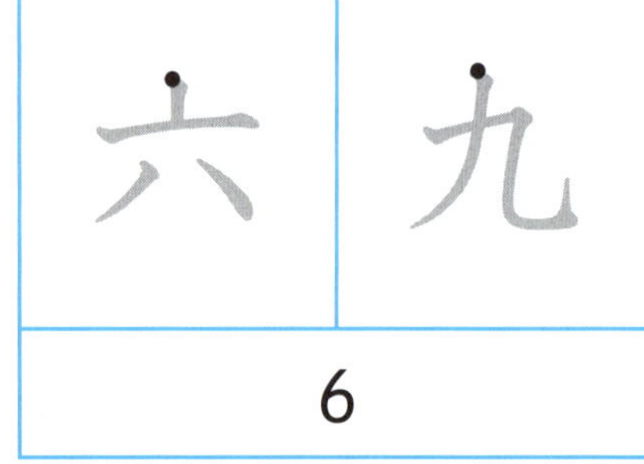
6

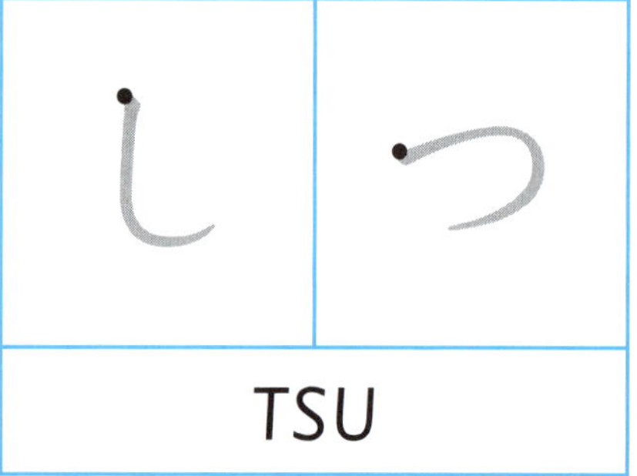
TSU

おおきい	big
ちいさい	small
まる	circle
しかく	square
さんかく	triangle

おかあさん	mother
おとうさん	father
わたしの	my (girls)
ぼくの	my (boys)
いえ	house

Trace over the correct Japanese word in your brightest colour.

my (boys)	わたしの　ぼくの　さんかく
father	おとうさん　いえ　さんかく
house	まる　いえ　ちいさい
triangle	しかく　ちいさい　さんかく
big	おおきい　まる　ちいさい
small	ちいさい　おおきい　いえ
mother	おとうさん　おかあさん
my (girls)	わたしの　ぼくの　さんかく
circle	いえ　まる　ぼくの

Trace over **one** letter in each box using your brightest colour, then follow your teacher's instructions.

REVISION BINGO		
し 六 へ	そ の 十	へ 四 八
三 る ひ	つ 九 く	一 五 て

ぶた	pig
うし	cow
いぬ	dog
うま	horse
ねこ	cat
ひつじ	sheep

☺☺☺ がすきです。	I like ☺☺☺.

ベッド	bed
ソファー	sofa
テレビ	TV

まど	window
ドア	door
テーブル	table

くるま	car
バス	bus
でんしゃ	train
じてんしゃ	bicycle

Trace over the correct Japanese word.

うま ねこ	バス でんしゃ	うま ひつじ
cat	train	horse
うし ぶた	がすきです じてんしゃ	でんしゃ くるま
pig	I like	car
ねこ いぬ	ひつじ じてんしゃ	いぬ まど
dog	sheep	window

Trace over **one** letter in each box using your brightest colour, then follow your teacher's instructions.

REVISION BINGO		
し 七 へ	ひ の 十	ん 四 八
三 六 ろ	る 九 て	二 五 く

LISTENING

Listen to the teacher, then circle the correct answer.

1
Japan Australia America

2
red yellow blue

3
9 7 3

4
black white red

5
2 8 10

Well Done!
You
remembered
◯
words.

READING

Look at the cards the teacher will show you. Circle the correct answer.

1
3 6 1

2
7 5 2

3
6 8 9

4
10 4 2

5
7 1 2

Well Done!
You
remembered
◯
words.

LISTENING

Listen to the teacher, then circle the correct answer.

1	2	3
head tummy legs	eyes ears mouth	skirt shirt dress

4	5
book pencil paper	chair desk teacher

Well Done!
You
remembered
words.

READING

Look at the cards the teacher will show you. Circle the correct answer.

1	2	3
3 4 8	SHI KU TE	NO TSU TE

4	5
TSU SO KU	NO KU TE

Well Done!
You
remembered
words.

HOW MUCH CAN YOU REMEMBER? LL 8–11; WL 1–8

LISTENING

Listen to the teacher, then circle the correct answer.

1	2	3
big small red	circle square triangle	mother father I

4	5
father my house blue	mother square big

Well Done! You remembered ◯ words.

READING

Look at the cards the teacher will show you. Circle the correct answer.

1	2	3
2 7 9	HE RO HI	HE RU RO

4	5
RO HI TSU	SHI KU HE

Well Done! You remembered ◯ words.

LISTENING

Listen to the teacher, then circle the correct answer.

1	2	3
pig house bed	sofa cat bus	cow horse dog

4	5
bus train car	bicycle pig train

Well Done! You remembered ◯ words.

READING

Look at the cards the teacher will show you. Circle the correct answer.

1	2	3
SO TSU N	KU SHI HE	NO RO N

4	5
SO TSU SHI	TE SO HI

Well Done! You remembered ◯ words.

